# ENDORSEMENTS

**THE WORSHIP UNICORN** SHOULD BE REQUIRED READING FOR EVERY WORSHIP LEADER, PASTOR, VOCALIST, BAND MEMBER, FRONT OF HOUSE, MEDIA, LIGHTING, STAGE CREW, USHER...ANYONE INVOLVED IN THE SERVICES AND GATHERINGS AT OUR CHURCHES TODAY. EACH CHAPTER IS A POWERFUL LESSON TO TAKE IN FOR TODAY'S LEVITE WHO IS BUSY CHASING THE PERFECT LEVEL OF WORSHIP TO HELP US ZERO IN ON THE THINGS THAT SHOULD MATTER THE MOST! I'M GOING TO PERSONALLY START INCLUDING DOUG'S BOOK IN ALL OF MY MENTORING FROM NOW ON.

JASON WHITEHORN // CCM ARTIST, WORSHIP PASTOR

IN **THE WORSHIP UNICORN** DOUG HOOD OFFERS A PRACTICAL, PERSONAL AND ENCOURAGING GUIDE FOR WORSHIP LEADERS WHO STRIVE TO ACHIEVE HIGHER EXCELLENCE IN THEIR MINISTRY. HE DOES SO NOT BY ADVISING MORE REHEARSAL OR SCRIPTING BUT BY LEADING A WORSHIP SERVICE WITH A PRAYERFUL HEART AND A CONTINUAL OPENNESS TO THE MOVEMENT OF THE HOLY SPIRIT. HE ALSO SHARES MOST CREDIBLY THAT THE USE OF TECHNOLOGY IS NOT THE FOCUS OF THE WORSHIP EXPERIENCE BUT RATHER ANOTHER TOOL MEANT TO CULTIVATE A RELATIONSHIP WITH THE LIVING GOD ... NAMELY IN THE PERSON OF JESUS CHRIST.

DEACON ROB JOSEPH // CATHOLIC DIOCESE OF COLUMBUS OH

DOUG HAS WRITTEN A BOOK THAT TAKES PRACTICAL INFORMATION AND PRESENTS IT IN AN INTRIGUING EASY-TO-READ FORMAT. IF YOU ARE LOOKING FOR GUIDANCE THAT HELPS TAKE YOUR WORSHIP TO THE NEXT LEVEL. THEN YOU MUST READ THIS BOOK!

**DAVID LEUSCHNER // DIGITAL GREAT COMMISSION MINISTRIES**

AS A VETERAN WORSHIP LEADER, I'M ALWAYS ON THE LOOKOUT FOR RESOURCES TO CHALLENGE AND INSPIRE, TO PULL ME OUT OF THE ROUTINE AND HELP ME LOOK IN THE MIRROR AND ASK THE DEEPER QUESTION, "AM I REALLY LEADING OUR CHURCH AND MINISTRY IN TRUE WORSHIP?" THIS BOOK AND DOUG'S KEEN OBSERVATIONS AND QUESTIONS, WILL HELP DEEPEN YOUR LEADERSHIP AND HEART FOR GOD AND HIS PEOPLE AND DEVELOP THE "ORIGINAL" APPROACH CRAFTED IN YOU TO DEEPEN YOUR WORSHIP PERSONALLY AND CORPORATELY. GET THIS BOOK! IT'S A TRUE "UNICORN" IN THE SEA OF WORSHIP RESOURCES.

**RICK STEWART // EXECUTIVE & WORSHIP PASTOR, NEW HOPE COMMUNITY CHURCH**

I CAN TESTIFY THAT DOUG HOOD IS A WORSHIP LEADER WHOSE HEART IS FOCUSED ON JESUS AND THE WORD. THE FACT THAT HE HAS TALENT, TECHNICAL PROWESS, AND CALMNESS IN FRONT OF AN AUDIENCE ONLY ENHANCES HIS ABILITY TO COMMUNICATE HIS HEART AND ENGAGE A CONGREGATION, ENCOURAGING THE PEOPLE TO EXPRESS THEMSELVES IN FREEDOM AND JOY IN A CHRIST-CENTERED WORSHIP EXPERIENCE. YOUNGER AND OLDER WORSHIP LEADERS ALIKE WOULD DO WELL TO DIGEST THE FUNDAMENTALS EXPRESSED IN **THE WORSHIP UNICORN**. THEY ARE WRITTEN BY A HUMBLE SERVANT-LEADER WHO SHARES A WEALTH OF KNOWLEDGE AND EXPERIENCE IN A STRAIGHT-FORWARD, HONEST, AND PRACTICAL WAY.

**DON WHARTON // SINGER, SONGWRITER, AUTHOR**

I HAVE HAD THE PRIVILEGE OF BEING LED BY DOUG IN WORSHIP FOR A DECADE. I HAVE NEVER MET A WORSHIP LEADER WHO IS BETTER AT BRINGING AN ENTIRE ROOM FULL OF MULTIGENERATIONAL BELIEVERS INTO THE PRESENCE OF GOD THAN DOUG. HE IS A ONE OF A KIND WORSHIP LEADER BECAUSE HIS HEART GENUINELY WANTS TO PLEASE GOD AND CONNECT PEOPLE TO THEIR CREATOR. IN A WORLD OF ENTERTAINMENT THAT HAS CREPT INTO SO MANY LARGE CHURCHES, THIS BOOK TEACHES YOU HOW TO EXPERIENCE THE PRESENCE OF THE SPIRIT AND AT THE SAME TIME GROW EXPONENTIALLY.

**JEREMY HELMUTH // SENIOR PASTOR, CENTRAL MINISTRIES**

**THE WORSHIP UNICORN** IS A BOOK FROM THE HEART OF, NOT ONLY A WORSHIP PASTOR BUT A WORSHIPPER. DOUG PUTS INTO WORDS WHAT MANY WORSHIP LEADERS AND PAS-TORS STRUGGLE AND DEAL WITH ON A WEEKLY BASIS, AND DOES SO IN A WAY THAT RES-ONATES DEEPLY AND REDIRECTS THE READER TO THE TRUTH OF THE GOSPEL AND THE ULTIMATE GOAL OF A WORSHIP LEADER/PASTOR, AND THAT IS TO DIRECT THE PEOPLE OF GOD TO THE THRONE OF GOD BY LEADING THROUGH MUSIC, SCRIPTURE AND THE ARTS. IF YOU ARE INVOLVED IN LEADING WORSHIP IN ANY CAPACITY, THIS IS A MUST-READ.

**CHRIS KUNTZ // WORSHIP PASTOR, HOPE MISSIONARY CHURCH**

# THE WORSHIP UNICORN

## TEN WAYS TO PURSUE AUTHENTIC & ENGAGING WORSHIP

## DOUGLAS JAMES HOOD

# DEDICATION

This book is dedicated to three very influential people in my life, three men whom I have had the privilege to work alongside in ministry, and in doing so, learned a great deal from each of them.

TO BRIAN GERIG: You first invited me to Central Ministries to be "the keyboard guy." I would have never guessed that nearly thirty years later, I would still be there. The time we spent together creating music was a valuable learning experience. Watching you lead, I started to get a glimpse of the heart of worship. We shared many (shall we say) "unique" moments together, and I'll always cherish those memories. When the time came for you to move on, I was honored that you asked me to take the baton and run ahead. I was full of hesitation and fear, but also knew it was right.

TO DON DELAGRANGE: I love your heart for people, I am impressed with the way you care for the church, and

I appreciate the many ways that we have been able to serve together over so many years. As the senior pastor, you were the one who had to deal with me as a young kid who really didn't know what he was doing. I appreciate the patience and grace that you extended. No doubt, I made a lot mistakes, but you were always an encourager, and you continue to support me to this day. I respect you a great deal. Thank you for being an excellent pastor and for shepherding God's people.

**TO JEREMY HELMUTH:** I've teamed up with you for more than ten years now. To say we've been through a lot is an understatement. I'm thankful that you place a high level of importance on worship. Our congregation is blessed to have a pastor who personally worships with them. I count it a privilege that we get to collaborate together every week to try to bring creativity and authenticity to the weekend worship experience. Over the years, we've seen God move in powerful ways as we as a church are obedient to His call. I'm grateful for your desire to see Him glorified and for your vision to keep on pursuing the Presence of the Lord in all we do.

# TABLE OF CONTENTS

# ACKNOWLEDGEMENTS

I would like to extend my heartfelt gratitude to all my church family at Central Ministries. We have worshipped together literally thousands of times. In reality, almost anything I've learned or have tried to un-learn, has happened in front of your very eyes. Words cannot describe how thankful I am that I am given the privilege to stand with you at least fifty-two times a year, as we all create an offering of worship and present ourselves to the Lord. I love that you bring me your real-life stories, you tell me how God is working, and you tell me your hurts and struggles. Thank you for being supportive, gracious, and passionate in worship.

**TO DAVID JOHNSON:** Thank you for bringing these thoughts and ideas to life. I'm grateful for the many ways I can collaborate with you, and watch you take a small seed of an idea and turn it into something big. You are a creative, and a visionary, who cares about telling stories with excellence. Thank you for helping to tell these stories.

**TO SARAH WESTFALL:** Thank you for pushing me to be better. I imagine working with the wrong editor could be filled with tension. I'm glad our working relationship together was never that way. In fact, I genuinely loved the way you would challenge me and stretch me to stay on point, to write more concisely, and ultimately deliver a better product. Thank for making this book a possibility.

**TO MY FAMILY (KIM, CADY, COOPER, KENDALL, EMMA, RILEY):** you've been a part of most of these stories. In my work life and church life, you've given me space to do what I love, and I love you for that. You see me at my best and at my worst, and you support me through it all. Living our lives together, smiling and laughing often, is a tremendous joy for me. You are my greatest treasure.

**TO THE BAND:** We often describe church as something we "get to" do and never something we "have to" do. No one outside our little group could probably ever understand how we operate. Our rehearsal structure is unusual, our preparation time is short, and my style of leading can be vague and hard to follow. I'm sure this is frustrating at times. Yet, you all remain faithful to the call. Not just to be great musicians. It's much deeper. I love the special bond we have, and it blows me away how God has honored our time together. The experiences we share every weekend are the highlight of my week. Thank you all for the way that you and your instrument make up our unique orchestra. Now, watch for my left foot to drop back...it's on! (band joke).

# FOREWORD

We live in a world where copying is the norm. Although, I'm old enough to remember how difficult it was for my elementary teachers to make copies of handouts. I can still remember that unique mimeograph smell like it was yesterday.

Then it got much easier to copy with the advent of bulky (at the time) Xerox photocopiers.

One lesson that was drilled into my psyche while studying graphic design in college: **be careful when copying!** Why? Because every copy you make always degrades quality. The tools that existed at the time caused the quality to decline until you had something unrecognizable. Of course, that was in the early days of photocopying and camera reproduction.

**Then the digital age changed everything.** I remember sitting down for the first time at a newly acquired MacIntosh computer at my first agency job. Grasping how it worked boggled my mind. I asked a team player, "how many times can you duplicate or copy a file before it degrades?" and he declared incredulously "it never does!"

A world of duplication, copying, and... stealing began. A world where counterfeiting was virtually undetectable.

Church worship, media, and communication has become saturated with knock-offs and replication. But unlike the digital world, it's back to the world where copying often degrades the quality.

As believers, who follow an amazing Creator, we are called to something better. A higher standard. And to uniqueness — a unicorn if you will.

What I've found in my decades of working with Church Leadership? I've discovered that those who strive to intertwine their unique giftedness and abilities into their ministries, and truly strive to create a unique world around them, are the ones that God uses to expand

His Kingdom. They are leaders rather than followers.

Sure it's easier to simply do it like all the others. Perhaps that's why we live in a world of influencers (people to emulate). Yet, God wants each of us to BE the influencer. And through the unique gifts He's infused into us, He wants us to uniquely add worth to His name, His Kingdom, and His power.

That is called genuine Worship.

The pursuit of finding your own uniqueness, can be daunting, kind of like chasing a unicorn. Don't feel unique? Feel like you copy more than create? Read on...

---

PERSONAL NOTE: I met Doug at the beginning of my quest to reach and teach the creative church world. He shaped my thinking, encouraged my actions, and set a foundation of where I am today. Because I copied him? No. See, he's a unicorn (humble, hardworking, talented, and big-hearted unicorn). And he challenged me to be one too. So I'm a different unicorn than Doug. That's the creative power that God the Creator has given us.

**Mark MacDonald**, Strategic Communication Catalyst (Florida Baptist Convention), Executive Director (Center For Church Communication), Bestselling Author (*Be Known For Something*)

# INTRODUCTION

I could probably give you at least one thousand reasons why I shouldn't be a worship leader. I'm not the greatest musician. I can be demanding, critical, and hard to follow. Sometimes the musical experiences I try to create fall far short of what I believe they could have been.

If you are a worship leader, you may have felt the same. Being a worship leader is much more than having the right qualifications or a certain degree of talent. If we don't have a heart for others, a real burden for the people we lead, and a true caring spirit for them as a shepherd cares for his flock, our music doesn't matter. Yes, we may be amazing musicians. Yes, people may applaud for us when the song has ended. But we can achieve all that and miss the mark. We may be a music director or a song leader, but in God's eyes, we might not be a worship leader.

Worship leaders have the responsibility of trying

to lead others into the presence of God. How can we be "ready" for that? I know for me personally, I never feel quite ready. I feel excited. I feel anxious. I even feel hopeful as we approach the weekend services and look forward to what the Lord is going to do. However, for me, every week as I prepare, I have a constant awareness of "How is it that God lets me do this?" Call it guilt, or call it humility—maybe a combination of both—but the awareness is certainly there.

Somewhere in our family scrapbook is an old picture of me in diapers raised up on my tippy toes to reach the keys of our family piano. Those eighty-eight keys have been a part of my life as long as I can remember. I started taking piano lessons at age seven at Fort Wayne Bible College in Fort Wayne, Indiana. Neither my parents nor I had any way of knowing then that years later, ironically, I would attend college there. What I did know was that I loved the piano, but I hated scales and hated practicing. I just wanted to play right away.

As a freshman in college, I played piano in the same practice rooms where I had learned to play scales as a seven-year-old boy. I walked the same corridors in Founder's Hall. The college later became Taylor University, where I graduated with a bachelor of science with a double major in music composition and Bible.

At some point in my life, in between piano lessons and graduation, I attended a service one evening at a local church. I don't remember why I was there, what the service was about, the sermon, or the songs. But I do remember a man sitting at a black grand piano, and he did more than sing and play the piano. He talked in between the songs. I didn't know it then, but this was my first introduction to seeing a worship leader in action. He was a worship leader before it was "cool" to be a worship leader. In fact, I don't know if the term *worship leader* had even been coined yet. It was before you had to have the "rock-star look." You know the stereotype: faux hawk, epic beard, skinny jeans, and tattoos. (I possess just one of the aforementioned. I'll let you guess.)

But there I sat, maybe thirteen years old, drawn to the authentic way this man spoke to the audience. I could see he was reaching people. He made an impact on others. I knew in that moment: *I want to do this.*

I've been behind a piano or a keyboard leading music for nearly thirty years now. But looking back, I realize that while I've led worship literally thousands of times, I've not always led true worship.

## LEADING AUTHENTIC WORSHIP OFTEN FEELS LIKE CHASING A UNICORN.

Did you know the Bible mentions unicorns nine times in the Kings James Version? Check it out for yourself Numbers 23:22, Numbers 24:8, Job 39:9, Job 39:10, Psalm 29:6, Psalm 92:10, Deuteronomy 33:17, Psalm 22:21, and Isaiah 34:7. Unicorns are commonly presented in movies, pictures, or art as a horse with a big horn coming out of its head. Though they don't exist today in that way, the King James Bible does in fact mention unicorns — an animal with one horn. Think of a rhinoceros. Actually, if you could find a two-hundred-year-old dictionary and look up the word *unicorn*, the definition says "rhinoceros." If you look up the word *rhinoceros,* the definition reads "unicorn."

Over the past two hundred years or so, our definition of a unicorn has morphed from the rhino to the more widely recognized mythical creature we now associate with that word. I suppose the idea and image of today's unicorn is just way more fun than the rhino.

And I can't say that I disagree. Unicorns are depicted as mysterious, elusive, intriguing, beautiful, and even magical—but something worth the chase. I feel the same about the pursuit of leading authentic, engaging worship.

Standing in the Lord's Presence is certainly wonderful and powerful. If we've been there, we want to go back, because we can think of no greater place we'd rather be. We yearn for more. We are hungry for those times when we look out and see people connecting to God through worship. We are no longer content with the average, the underwhelming, the ordinary "rhinos." We want that unicorn.

But many weeks, our services don't match our expectations. We look out and observe not enough singing, not enough participation, not enough connection. In those moments, we can easily wonder whether we will ever catch that unicorn again.

If we're not careful, we can get sidetracked or derailed. We can easily slip up, focusing on things that don't matter or even things that we never should have pursued. We compare ourselves to other leaders and other churches. We chase after concepts and ideas that might be appropriate for others, but not for us.

### BUT THE WORLD HAS ENOUGH COPIES.
### YOU ARE CALLED TO BE AN ORIGINAL.

The purpose of this book is to help you become just that. For worship leaders who are starting out, I want to encourage you to start right. For the leaders who have a few years under their belts, I want to challenge you and push you to be better. Not in terms of talent (yes, that is important), but by digging deep into your worship DNA and developing *your* way of leading worship that is unique to *you*. We are all wired to do things differently, and YOU are wired to do something amazing. The trick is to find your way and be comfortable with that.

In this book, I give you ten tools to discover and develop who you are as a worship leader. As you explore your leadership style, you can uncover a mysterious yet wonderful blend of comfort, vulnerability, and confidence. You can better connect and lead your congregation. Each chapter closes with an easy-to-understand idea that you can apply in the church you serve now or the church you will serve in the future. My goal is to help you lead more effectively than ever before.

If you chase after God and if you truly pursue His heart with the persistent, relentless prayer of "God help me lead these people in the way You want me to," I believe you will learn their worship language and you will discover what resonates with them. When you do this, you get to be along for the ride on a beautiful journey, watching God do powerful things through you for the sake of His Kingdom.

CHASE THE UNICORN. BE RELENTLESS.

IT'S MYSTERIOUS, POWERFUL, AND WONDERFUL.

AND IT'S WORTH THE PURSUIT.

xxx

# 1

## MUSIC IS NOT WORSHIP

### THINK LIKE A LEADER, NOT JUST A MUSICIAN

I began playing piano at age seven, and by the time I was the ripe old age of eleven, I was playing at church. I was the kid they would prop up on the piano for church offertory. I loved it. And through the years that would expand into playing synthesizer and even occasionally a duet with the organ players—either Rod or Paul. I remember Pastor Prosser giving me a hymnal. Inside it, he wrote, "Always play for Him." I never forgot that. I will always cherish those memories.

Believe it or not, in high school I was also a member of a rap group where I wrote the music, programmed the drum loops, and sequenced all the instruments. It was a time of great creativity in a different genre and I made fun memories with my best friend Dan. Mix in some Johnny Cash, Billy Joel, Journey, The Art of Noise, Depeche Mode, Duran Duran, Genesis, and Tears for Fears, and you can get a taste of the musical soundtrack of my life. My first introduction to a thing called contemporary Christian music was from my new girlfriend Kim (now my wife), who I met my freshman year of college. I soon became familiar with new artists like Steve Camp, Whiteheart, Michael Card, Bryan Duncan, Phil Keaggy, and a keyboard player I really connected with named Michael W. Smith.

It was during this time, my freshman year of college, where I began to lead music, specifically lead others in song during our daily chapel services. If you were to look at me then, I looked like the guy I had seen leading worship in a local church years earlier. I was sitting at a black grand piano, singing and playing. I was making music. I was leading a band. The people in the audience were singing. I suppose you could make the case that technically I was leading worship, but I don't think I was, at least not consistently. Yes, I was leading a band, and yes, we were leading others in song, but my brain was in the wrong place. My thoughts were all about the music. My thoughts were on musical excellence. My thoughts were on the musical experience and the skill level of the band. I was totally unaware that we could deliver an amazing musical experience that was spiritually dead.

### I THOUGHT GOOD MUSIC WAS ENOUGH. IT'S NOT.

I'm convinced that I have led worship services that were full of noise. I never intentionally set out to do that, but I'm sure it has happened. Why? Because of my heart, my attitude, my thoughts. When these things are in the wrong place, as Amos says, God doesn't even hear my melody.

*I hate, I despise your religious festivals;*
*your assemblies are a stench to me.*

*Even though you bring me burnt offerings*
*and grain offerings, I will not accept them.*
*Though you bring choice fellowship offerings,*
*I will have no regard for them.*
*Away with the noise of your songs!*
*I will not listen to the music of your harps.*
*(Amos 5:21–23)*

In this example, God sees a big production but is not impressed. I imagine the people who attended these religious festivals and assemblies were having quite a good time at what would have been an important and well-attended social event for the community. In my imagination, I picture signs and banners, vendors with their fares on display for purchase, delicious food, and lots of socializing. No doubt someone was doing a Facebook Live feed.

Looking at these assemblies as an attendee, I would have been impressed. I'm convinced that much impresses us, but not God. For this reason, this passage blows my mind. We can pursue the physical so hard that we completely blow the spiritual. Specifically, we can have one hundred percent success in the technicalities and have zero percent success in the hearts of people. Even in the moments where our melodies are amazing and people applaud and we feel like we've played a song in a Grammy Award–winning way, if our brains are in the wrong place, all we've created to God's ear is noise.

If I were to offer my "Doug Translation Bible" on this passage, it would go something like this: "I will not hear the melody of thy awesome five-octave voice, nine-string bass, eleven guitar pedals, twenty-four tracks of stems, ferocious Leslie B3 organ, twenty-five-piece custom drum kit, or world's most expensive and exotic custom acoustic guitar carved out of one solid piece of wood from a one-thousand-year-old tree."

The point here is that we place importance on musical abilities, stage presence, outward appearance, and technical excellence—sometimes more than the heart. We impress people with things that don't impress God. Lest I be misunderstood, let me emphasize we *can* use all these things to God's glory if our motives, intent, and hearts are in the right place. That would be awesome! But if our motives, intent, and hearts are disconnected from the Lord, He won't even hear our melody.

### CAN MUSIC BE WORSHIP? YES.
### IS ALL MUSIC WORSHIP? NO.

As I've grown as a leader I've learned to value participation more than perfection. However, the challenge is that people can participate in many ways. Some are visible. Some are not. As a leader, I can fall into the trap of judging with my physical eyes how much or how little people are participating. And I can transfer that "success" or "failure" onto myself as a leader. I shouldn't do that.

At the core of authentic worship is our ability to let our hearts explode in response to God. For some people, that inward explosion manifests itself in an outward expression that others can see. For some, that inner explosion is almost totally contained deep inside. You might see a tear, you might see lips quiver when they sing, but you won't see an overtly demonstrative type of expression. And you know what? That's okay.

Some worshippers need to hear that it's okay if they are not very expressive by nature. Others need to hear the message that it's okay if they *are* expressive by nature. Everyone should be able to find freedom in worship. I've talked to people who think they are weird because it's natural for them to raise their hands and dance during worship. They feel singled out because they are too expressive. I've talked to people who think their worship is somehow worth less, because they stand quietly and are more reflective as they worship. They feel singled out because they don't raise their hands and they don't dance. We must allow both extremes to exist in the same room. I don't think God created us to be robotic, predictable, and always similar in our worship. We should not lift a person up if they are very expressive, and equally we should not push a person down if they are more reserved. Consider 1 Samuel 16:7: "People look at the outward appearance, but the LORD looks at the heart."

I think the key here is to recognize and appreciate that we have true freedom to express ourselves in worship the way God wired us. We may differ in terms of personality, family tradition, denominational heritage, and musical preference. Yet, Scripture is full of biblical examples that show us acceptable ways to worship. We can look at these expressions of worship not only in terms of what is acceptable, but also in terms of what can aspire.

Ready for some controversy? Here we go. As leaders, or congregations, although we would probably all say we believe in the Bible, we appear to have selective memory, or maybe more accurately selective belief on Bible verses. Consider this passage from Psalm 63:

*You, God, are my God,*
*earnestly I seek you;*
*I thirst for you,*
*my whole being longs for you,*
*in a dry and parched land*
*where there is no water.*
*I have seen you in the sanctuary*

*and beheld your power and your glory.*

*Because your love is better than life,*

*my lips will glorify you.*

*I will praise you as long as I live,*

*and in your name I will lift up my hands.*

*I will be fully satisfied as with the richest of foods;*

*with singing lips my mouth will praise you. (v. 1–5)*


The passage starts out fairly harmless: "God, earnestly I seek you." I think, "*Yes, I believe that. I feel good about that.*" I read the next phrase: "I have seen you..." I still feel good. I love to walk around in nature. I enjoy observing creation, and I believe God made it all. I'm drawn to God as I take in the world around me. But here is where things start to unravel for many worship leaders: "And in your name I will lift my hands."

Though the Bible tells us raising hands to God is a good thing, this little phrase has been powerful enough to cause sane people to go crazy. We argue. We end relationships. We might even leave a church over raising our hands. How on earth could this be? Does this passage mean raising hands is a matter of salvation? No. Does it mean we all need to do it? Nope. Can we go to heaven if we never raise our hands during our entire lives? Yes. Does it mean it is a good and valuable way to express ourselves when we pray and worship? Yes. Should we extend a bit more grace to those who are wired to be more outwardly expressive in their worship? Probably.

And just so we don't blame this on some fancy new translation, let's go back and look at the good ol' King James Version:

*O God, thou art my God; early will I seek thee: my soul thirsteth for thee, my flesh longeth for thee in a dry and thirsty land, where no water is; to see thy power and thy glory, so as I have seen thee in the sanctuary. Because thy lovingkindness is better than life, my lips shall praise thee. Thus will I bless thee while I live: I will lift up my hands in thy name. My soul shall be satisfied as with marrow and fatness; and my mouth shall praise thee with joyful lips*

*[...] (Psalm 63:1–5 KJV)*

Raising hands is an interesting subject. Sometimes I wonder "God, why is this even an issue?" What if, instead, the Bible would have instructed us in true Arthur Fonzarelli style to raise our thumbs up during worship? Or hop on our right legs? What if as a sign of appreciation for a song we would wink one eye? What if when we were truly engaged in worship, and completely immersed in the power of God's presence, that we would blink both eyes quickly? Would the blinkers be deemed as more spiritual than the winkers? Is there anything else that could have been described that wouldn't get people so worked up? Probably not. People are crazy. People create drama. We tend to get all riled up about things that don't really matter. (I'll purposely not mention the topics of dance, flags, tongues, and so on to prevent a full-fledged riot.)

Leading our bands, vocalists, ensembles, and choirs with excellence is definitely important. We should always strive to give our absolute best. We are called to that, right here in the book of Psalms: "Sing to him a new song; play skillfully, and shout for joy" (33:3).

But I'm also aware of this truth: You can create

musical excellence onstage and look out to a sea of people who are disconnected, unengaged, and (spiritually speaking) dead. If we excel at music, but we do not make an authentic connection to those we lead, we fall short. We should be driven to passionately pursue those connections, find out what unites us, and then creatively lead in a language and style (perhaps even raising hands) in order to reach those people God puts in front of us.

As we rehearse each week before the people arrive, we stand on our stages during sound check and look out to empty seats. Depending on your venue, you may have pews, theatre seats, or even stackable chairs. Pray for those seats. Every week God will bring in tens, hundreds, or thousands of people and plop them down right in front of you. These people are souls. Don't look at them as an audience. Worship is not a gig. As a worship leader, you have the awesome, heavy responsibility to speak truth and encouragement into these souls. Sunday is never "just another Sunday." It could be someone's last chance. He might be walking through your doors asking God to give him some kind of glimpse into why he should go on with his life. You just might be that voice.

# ACTION

THE NEXT TIME YOU LEAD, BE KEENLY AWARE OF YOUR THOUGHTS. ARE YOU THINKING ONLY AS A MUSICIAN OR AS A WORSHIP LEADER? ASK GOD TO OPEN YOUR SPIRITUAL EYES AND EARS TO BE IN TUNE TO WHAT THE HOLY SPIRIT IS DOING AMONG THE PEOPLE. BE DETERMINED TO HONOR GOD WITH YOUR HEART NO MATTER HOW AWESOME OR UNDERWHELMING THE MUSIC IS.

# 2

# YOU ARE THE POTTER & GOD IS THE CLAY

## DON'T WRITE YOUR OWN SCRIPT

Wait a minute. I messed up the chapter title, right? Shouldn't it read "God is the potter and we are the clay" (see Isaiah 64:8)? Hang with me.

In my business, I'm fortunate to travel across the country and see how many churches approach service planning. I've seen all the extremes: the church with one hour of music, the church that does three total songs, the church that does one song for thirteen minutes, the fifteen-minute sermon, the two-hour sermon. We certainly have many flavors of the way we do church.

The duration of any particular service element doesn't concern me as much as how we treat those self-induced time constraints. Yes, I said it: We do this to ourselves. The struggle with how much time to give God is a self-inflicted issue that we have created. God did not put us in a clock box. We created it, and we jumped inside. Imagine back in Bible times when people went to pray. I seriously doubt that any of the disciples said "Okay, let's have only one of you lead out today, because we're running late."

Far more often than we care to admit, we are lured into writing the script for our worship experiences, and we wait for God to follow. Of course, we never consciously take that stance, and we would never put that in writing as how we approach our Sunday planning. But nonetheless, it happens. We become rigid and unmovable for the sake of organization, planning, and logistics. Today, we have innovative and helpful planning tools, apps, and online software, all of which are designed to keep us organized and streamline communications with our teams.

I use them too. These resources have some great benefits for sure. But the danger I see, and the caution I share, is that we need to leave room for God to move, in the way He chooses, and on His time schedule.

Healthy worship leaders continually invite God to rule and reign in their services. Can God lead us when we are planning weeks ahead? Sure. He can certainly give us specific ideas and creative ways to stitch together a worship service. The Lord can lead in lots of details, and He can give us insights as we plan. But we should also be willing to throw all that out the window if the Holy Spirit decides to move in a different direction while the service is already happening. In fact, I would dare go as far as to say we should crave that very thing. I know I do.

Consider what that flexibility during worship might look like: Maybe the Holy Spirit moves powerfully in the second song of the worship set, and He wants you to remain in that song for an extended period. Maybe God leads you to pray over your congregation during the third song. Maybe some truth is revealed in a very personal way for your church during the first song, and the pastor needs to come up and expound upon it, to teach the church what he is sensing from God in that moment. Maybe you are supposed to do more worship at the end of the service rather than the beginning. All these variations from the plan (and more) are very real possibilities.

Here's the rub: How do we respond internally when we sense that God is on the move, but the clock says we are thirty seconds over? As worship leaders, that tension is real. Churches have all kinds of clever ways to tell the worship leader or the pastor they have gone too long and are over their time limit. I've seen it all. Interesting hand signals. Handwritten cue cards. Flashing red lights. Messages on a screen. Countdown timers. The list goes on and on. Again, none of these in and of themselves are necessarily bad. But, I would go so far as to say that many life-changing worship moments have died because we were afraid to go off script.

Now, don't misunderstand and think that I am anti-technology or that I think every service should be a wild, unplanned adventure with no sense of order or purpose. I use the latest software to plan worship every week. In fact, I'm an app junkie. Gone are the days of flipping through a binder or pieces of paper on a music stand. Each Sunday, my iPad is synced to my online planning platform, all my songs are loaded, I can transpose to any key, and I love it all. These tools are incredible! I love the way that these programs give worship leaders a better experience. But we must remember that we are not in control, and to the extent that we remind ourselves of that, we invite God into every service. And as we genuinely welcome the Holy Spirit to direct our days, I know greater things can and will happen.

Church congregations can connect today in ways we couldn't even dream up just a few years ago. And that's a good thing! But adding solid technical connections while maintaining a freedom for the Holy Spirit to move freely can be quite a challenge.

For example, not too long ago, if I was leading a service that had more of a free flow to it, I would just print out a bunch of chord charts, have them on the music stand, and flip through them to whatever song I needed. I would start to play a few bars, and the band could pick up where I was going and follow along.

If I were to lead that same service today, different thoughts run through my mind. Now, if I want to make a song change, these real thoughts race through my mind in a matter of microseconds:

*Do we have the lyrics loaded into the graphics computer?*
*If not, will the vocalists know the words?*
*Will this song gel with the lighting cues already planned?*
*Where is my phone? Can I text the front-of-house engineer?*
*Will the broadcast and camera team get the message?*
*Will this throw off the ushers to come up for the offering?*
*Does the bass guitarist have a printed-off sheet of this?*
*Does the acoustic guitar need to capo?*
*I don't have a click track. Will the drummer be okay?*

In fairness, some tools give the worship leader more freedom in going back and repeating a chorus (for example), but we still face limitations to abandoning the plans for the day and doing something different.

We must establish a balance between technical and musical excellence and the freedom to follow God's prompting. If we take the time and invest our efforts, we can find that balance. It will look different for each of us, so we have to devote ourselves to taking the time to pray and seek God out in these matters. God's prerequisites for worship might be different than ours. But if we ask for wisdom in this area, He will give it.

I remember a Sunday during the Christmas season when I experienced one of the most vivid examples of contrast ever. Our sermon theme was on how to approach God. During the first service, Pastor Jeremy started out with several minutes of silence as many thought-provoking statements and questions were displayed on the video screens.

Everything during the first service went "as planned." However, we got quite a surprise (especially me) when during the second service when right in the middle of worship, we lost all power. The outage was not just a blown fuse (which we had experienced before) but was affecting the entire building and large portion of the surrounding community. The power was out.

I suddenly found myself as the worship leader with everything stripped away. No music, no instruments, no projectors, no lights—nothing left but people in a very dark room. This sudden change was a big surprise to us, but not to God. He knew it would happen. In advance, He had prompted me to have the song "God Is So Good" in the worship set that day. We moved into that song, singing several verses with just our voices. It was beautiful.

Pastor Jeremy came up next and delivered a modified version of the same message he had delivered during the first service, but without the visual aids. It was a great message from the heart. Several people responded with first-time decisions for Christ. What could be better?

At the close of the sermon, the worship team and I took the stage and sang "Amazing Grace (My Chains Are Gone)." The worship team later asked me why I didn't have the acoustic guitar play, or grab some Latin percussion. After all, our nature (at least mine) is to try and fix things when they go wrong. But in that moment, I felt that things had not gone wrong. God had pulled the plug on us, and we needed to honor that change and stay totally unplugged. We closed the service with this beautiful scene: hundreds of people standing, some eyes closed, some hands raised, all singing this simple, yet powerful song acapella.

Fast forward three hours later that same day. I attended the Christmas show from Trans-Siberian Orchestra along with ten thousand of my closest friends. If you're not familiar with this group, they put on one of the most technically advanced shows out there. As someone in the audio/visual and lighting business, I am SO jealous of the gear these guys have.

Yet when I watched the show that afternoon, I contrasted what the Trans-Siberian Orchestra had with what we were a part of earlier that morning in church. There was no comparison. Although I was deeply jealous of the funds they had at their disposal to use the arts in a creative way, the show that day felt empty to me. Why? Because I had experienced the power of God's presence in a pure and completely honest way just a few hours prior.

I thank God for showing me this contrast, for showing up at our services in powerful ways. I still would like multiple semitrucks full of audio/visual and lighting equipment like Trans-Siberian Orchestra, but in the meantime, I invite Him to pull the plug on us anytime He wants.

## ACTION

ASK YOURSELF: IS THERE ANY WAY GOD MIGHT WANT TO PULL THE PLUG AT MY CHURCH? BE OPEN TO LETTING HIM SHAKE THINGS UP, AND WAIT FOR GOOD THINGS TO HAPPEN. ANTICIPATE CHANGE. IF YOU FIND YOURSELF IN A SITUATION THAT COMES AS A SURPRISE TO YOU, TRY TO REST IN THAT. RESIST THE URGE TO FIX IT. LET GOD BE THE CAPTAIN, AND GO ALONG FOR THE RIDE.

# 3

# FACTS VS STORIES

## CONNECT WITH PEOPLE

When we tell stories, we tend to speak to people more deeply than if we just share facts. Information is important. Facts and figures can help reinforce an idea. They can provide compelling data. But nothing resonates with people like a good, true story—and the Bible is full of them.

I've also watched God write numerous stories in my church. One of my earliest memories regarding the power of worship involves a story about a lady named Lu. Lu had an outgoing personality; she was super positive, genuinely encouraging, and very enthusiastic in her worship. Long before I knew her personally, I noticed her out in the congregation singing with passion. From the look on her face, her countenance would tell you she loved to worship the Lord. She was the depiction of Psalms 34:5, which says "Those who look to him are radiant; their faces are never covered with shame."

One other thing about Lu: She was in a wheelchair. I didn't know the details about why she was in the chair, but as I got to know Lu and her caring friend Sherry, they would both speak uplifting words to me. (Even today, years later, I still see these ladies every week, and they continue to be a source of encouragement and support.) But when I was getting to know Lu, I was struck with the seemingly conflicting reality that even though Lu was in a wheelchair, she was always so positive, so cheerful. She was thankful and vocal in giving her praise to God.

As the worship leader, I thought "We need some of her energy on stage so others can see it!" In those days, our facility seated approximately 250 or so on the floor with additional seating in the balcony. You've likely seen this church setup before: a traditional-style sanctuary with an A-frame roof and wood-beam ceiling. Built in the early 1970s, the space was nice, with a modest-sized stage. Like most buildings of that era, accessibility was limited, so while I wanted to bring Lu up on stage, we had no ramp or path to push a wheelchair up. Still, I felt strongly that Lu needed to be up in front on that platform.

I approached a few guys and asked whether they would help lift Lu (in her wheelchair) up and down the stage on the weeks that she sang. They agreed. Was it a little awkward? Yes. It was not a smooth transition in the service. I worried what it looked like. I wondered whether it was a distraction. Most weeks, I would pray after the last song of the main set and then walk over along with my friends Jeff, Craig, or Curt, and we would pick up Lu and carry her down to the main floor level. I can still hear her whispering "Thanks guys" every week when we set her down. Looking back now, since I've become so focused on smooth transitions, I'm honestly amazed that we did it. The logistical part of me today would probably try and argue many ways why we could not do it. But I believed then it was important—and it was.

Here's why: In that same general timeframe, God was working in me not be content with "regular worship." Because of the time constraints of a Sunday morning, the format did not allow us to rest in His presence as much as He would like, nor as much as we needed. I was hungry for more, and fifteen-minute worship segments were not cutting it.

Coming out of this awareness, we started to develop the idea of a Saturday night worship service. The agenda was pretty simple: extended worship. Our church had never done anything like this, so we knew it was a risk. We began to get the word out using an amazing technology for the day (postcards and stamps) to tell everyone. We planned to do this worship service one Saturday every month to see whether we could give people an outlet to go deeper in their personal worship. And frankly, we also hoped this desire for deeper worship would spill over into our Sunday mornings. It did. In fact today, when I look at the expressive nature of our Sunday-morning experience, I realize that in some ways, the way we worship now was birthed in what we then called Saturday night worship.

During one such Saturday night, I was leading, and things were moving along as usual. We were in the middle of a song, and I was playing and singing with my eyes closed as I often do. I heard some movement around me, so I opened my eyes and saw someone standing near me at eye level. That someone was Lu.

For as long as I'd known her, when I talked to Lu, I was talking "down" to her as she sat in her wheelchair approximately three or four feet above the ground. But in that moment, to see her at eye level, face to face, was just flat-out bizarre. My thoughts quickly turned from "Hey, this is weird!" to "Wait a minute... Lu just got healed!" Right in the middle of worship, Lu got up and walked. And not only did she walk, but she walked up on stage— the same stage where we had carried her so many times. Our Pastor Don came up and helped guide us through that moment. That service was powerful, one that I'll never forget. God is still in the miracle business. This is the God to whom we sing.

If you look around your church, I bet you have many stories about what God is doing among your congregation. When you stand on your stage and you tell a story to the people, remind them that this is a real-life story, of real-life people, who are in that room, sitting beside them at that very moment. People will take notice and listen. Talk about how God is still in the business of working miracles. Remind people that God is alive and well and is still writing stories amongst them.

To find these stories, you need to know your people. You have to do more than stand on stage and be a musician. You are called to be a leader, a shepherd. A shepherd knows his sheep. As leaders, we need to have relationships with people that don't involve us standing on a stage with a spotlight on us and them watching. We need real, relational interactions where we are on equal ground. This type of connection can happen over coffee, doughnuts, pastries, dessert (yes, I have a major sweet tooth), but whatever the setting, make relationships a priority.

Social media is also an excellent way to get a pulse on your church community. I'll often ask people to share what's happening in their lives. Or I'll ask: What are they needing in worship? How are they trusting God? What do they need from God? Facebook, Twitter, and Instagram are powerful platforms to do this. Not only can you capture the information you want, but others with whom you or your church are connected through social media can see the testimonials too.

Whether face to face or online, the pursuit is for connection. When we connect better, two wonderful things will happen. First, the people you lead will see you on a different level as their leader. They will understand your heart more, feel closer to you, and most likely be better connected to you as you lead them in worship. I've found that when people can see me as just a "regular guy" they also listen better during those moments when I'm trying to minister to them. Secondly, as you are leading, and you visually scan out across your congregation, you will be better connected to them. It's a natural byproduct of your investment in them. You know their lives, their struggles, and their victories in greater detail. All this connection contributes toward a deeper sense of community.

As we know each other more, we have a more powerful worship offering. We present ourselves to the Lord, raise our voices, and give our songs to Him as a united worship sound pleasing to His ears.

# ACTION

LOOK FOR A STORY ABOUT HOW GOD HAS MOVED IN THE LIFE OF SOMEONE IN YOUR CHURCH. DON'T WORRY HOW IMPRESSIVE OR CLEVER THE STORY IS. SEARCH FOR A GENUINE WAY GOD HAS SHOWN HIS POWER, AND THEN TELL THAT STORY IN AN HONEST, AUTHENTIC WAY DURING THE MIDDLE OF YOUR WORSHIP SET. PRACTICE TELLING THE STORY SO IT'S JUST TWO MINUTES LONG, AND FRAME THE NARRATIVE IN A WAY WHERE ALL THE CREDIT AND ATTENTION GOES TO GOD. WHEN YOU'RE DONE, TRANSITION INTO A SONG THAT SHARES THE THEME OF THE STORY. WATCH OTHERS BE DRAWN INTO THE STORY AND THE SONG TAKE ON NEW MEANING.

# 4

## INVISIBLE GENIUSES

### DON'T MISS TALENT RIGHT IN YOUR FACE

For most, if not all churches, volunteers are the lifeblood of our weekend services. They unlock buildings, set up chairs, greet people in the parking lot, teach classes, serve coffee, hand out bulletins, help people find seats, pass out offering plates, change diapers, operate sound systems, display song lyrics, create and cue lighting scenes, and much more. Depending on your church, you may relate to a handful of these roles or all of them, but either way, I'm certain you rely on volunteers. These people serve, some every week, for years at a time for zero pay and little recognition. They are important to the church, and they should be important to us. Not because we need them to fill a slot in a rotation, but because they are people first. God loves them, and we need to love them. If we miss them, we can miss tremendous talent—like Vince.

Vince[1] was the son of a preacher; it was natural for him to want to be like his dad, so he went to seminary. However, Vince wasn't a good student or a strong public speaker. Even so, after completing seminary, he took the job of pastor for a church in Belgium. The mining-town community was poor, and he connected with the plight of the people. He observed them. He began to draw the people and the surroundings of his town.

After a short six months, his deficient preaching skills caught up with him, and his role as a paid pastor ended. Vince tried to continue on his own, remaining for a short while unpaid, but eventually he gave up and left the church. It is said he never set foot in a church again.

But while he was there, Vince made a real connection with people of the village. He watched them. He painted them—his talent for painting far outweighing his talent for preaching. He went on to create several paintings containing landscapes and scenes of buildings, houses, and churches.

In what would become one of his most famous works, Vincent van Gogh painted *Starry Night* in 1889, one year before his death. While his paintings were beautiful even at a quick glance, they were also insightful upon closer inspection. Here's what I observe: The windows of the houses all have candles. Each house is lit. All the buildings have light coming from the windows—except the church. The church remains dark and unlit. Perhaps, to Vince, the church was a cold, dark, unwelcoming place. After all, that had been his experience.

After he left the church, the rest of his life was described as extreme emotional, relational, and financial turmoil. He grew despondent and hopeless. At the age of thirty-seven, he took a gun and ended his own life. Vincent van Gogh is now recognized throughout the world as one of the most talented painters and artists of all time. The world now lifts him up on a pedestal for all to see. They recognize his talent and pay huge sums of money to purchase what he created. Ironically, the small church in

Belgium didn't see that invisible genius. They had no use for him and instead threw him away. Imagine how this story could have ended differently.

**THINK ABOUT YOUR CHURCH.**

**WOULD AN ARTIST CHOOSE TO SHARE**

**HIS OR HER TALENTS AT YOUR CHURCH?**

I wonder how many invisible geniuses are in our churches right now. People who are incredibly gifted in a way we have not yet noticed. Chances are we as the church have a need, and they as an individual have a gift to give. As you strive to lead your people better and chase the worship unicorn, your teams are a vital part of that pursuit. Vocalists, instrumentalists, audio engineers, graphic designers, lighting programmers, camera operators—all these people help to create the worship experience.

Be on the lookout for how you can best utilize people's gifts and get them plugged in within your church.

Identify people's strengths, passions, and talent. Take those attributes and make a connection point with an area of ministry within your church.

Your story could go something like this: "Hey Steve, it seems like helping with announcements isn't a good fit for you, but we have seen your amazing graphic design work. Would you be interested in helping create visuals for Sunday?" Or, "Hey Bob, you have such an energetic personality and you connect so well with others; we're wondering if you would consider serving on our hospitality and greeter team, instead of singing on the worship team?"

When people are living in the unique ways God has made them, their lives and your church body can be living out true life of worship. Then, you can stand back and watch amazing kingdom work happen.

# ACTION

SEARCH THROUGH YOUR CIRCLE OF INFLUENCE, THE PEOPLE WITH WHOM YOU COME IN CONTACT. LOOK FOR PEOPLE WHO MIGHT FEEL INVISIBLE OR MIS-PLACED. FIND AN AREA WHERE THEY COULD SERVE AUTHENTICALLY AND FIND FULFILLMENT. PLUG THEM IN AND SPEAK INTENTIONAL WORDS OF ENCOUR-AGEMENT TO THEM. AND IF THAT MEANS MOVING THEM FROM THE PULPIT TO THE PAINTBRUSH, THEN SO BE IT.

# 5

## WHEN HONESTY HURTS

### DON'T LET WORDS KILL WORSHIP

I am active in a group called the National Association of Church Design Builders (NACDB). The NACDB is a group of professionals throughout the United States who design and build churches. At one of our meetings recently, the question was asked: "What is something you really value in others?" We went around the room, and people gave some answers you could expect, such as honor, reliability, trust, dependability, and other stuff like that. My friend Ravi gave a different perspective, one that stood out and has stuck with me. He responded something like this: "Tell me the truth, but tell it to me in a way I can hear." This perspective is so powerful. Let me explain why.

You probably know people who say things like "I just tell it like it is" or "I'll be cut and dry." My translation for what they really mean goes something like this: "I will be honest and if I hurt your feelings or crush you as a person in the process, so be it." Now, I doubt whether anyone would really admit that my translation accurately describes them, but we all know this form of "truth-telling" happens and is extremely hurtful. People can be destroyed with just one word. Damage made in an instant can be devastating, taking months or years to heal. In some cases, the relationship never mends, and the wound remains. Can we be brutally honest, without being brutal?

**WE CANNOT DESTROY OTHERS AND LEAD WORSHIP.**

Sadly, we see this type of communication in the church.

We see it within worship teams. We see it between worship leader and band and between band and the sound engineer. We see it with the senior pastor talking to the person operating the lyrics computer. Hurtful words are terrible and should not happen. Let me phrase this stronger: They CANNOT happen. We cannot use our tongues to destroy others and then with the same tongue try to give an inspiring sermon or lead a heartfelt worship experience. James 3:10 says, "Out of the same mouth come praise and cursing. My brothers and sisters, this should not be."

We can also hurt each other when we talk about worship—both in person and online. Have you seen all the worship rants happening on social media? One party touts that all contemporary worship is bad, while another boldly states that all modern worship is great but hymns are no longer relevant. Other criticisms love to crop up: How loud is too loud? Have theatrical lighting systems become too showy, poisoning the worship experience? Do we sing too many new songs? Not enough songs? Too many old songs? People take sides, and the conversation quickly becomes all-or-nothing. No one is in it to listen.

I wish we could all take a collective breath, calm down, hold hands by a campfire, hug it out, sing "Friends," and have a good cry. (Okay, maybe I'm being a little dramatic...) But we need some realistic perspective to this conversation. We need to be able to have different opinions, realize style preferences exist, and leave it at that. I have a newsflash for you: You can, in fact, disagree, yet do so in a polite way where people remain friends. Let's do more of that.

## MUSIC PREFERENCE IS JUST THAT—A PREFERENCE.
## LET'S CHOOSE OUR BATTLES.

If your words are outwardly threatening and hurtful, then people will not hear your message. In that moment, you also reveal the true state of your heart, "for the mouth speaks what the heart is full of" (Luke 6:45).

One time a few years ago, I did something I had

not done since I was a little kid. I got down on my knees and prayed. Not figuratively speaking, but the real deal. I actually got down on the floor to pray. It was hard to do. My back had been bothering me with severe pain, so getting on the floor was physically hard. I found it good though.

Many cultures today kneel as a means of greeting or even as part of their religious traditions. Most of us in the United States find kneeling to be out of the norm. The Bible, however, is full of people kneeling before God. But why? When people kneel, they take a posture of submission and/or reverence. Should this not also be our spiritual posture when we pray?

I found it ironic that it was on that day, when I could barely move (due to my back trouble), God prompted me to get on the floor. And as I knelt, with my face down, I did the things we are to do when we pray. I confessed sins. I asked for healing. I told God that He was good and I loved Him. My prayers seemed to mean a little more on my knees. As I rose from the floor, although my muscles quivered in pain, I felt stronger. The things I gained by kneeling in prayer were much greater than just a quick physical healing.

What if you were to get down on your knees and bring your congregation before the Lord? What if you asked God to show you what they need? How might that change your heart, let alone the words you speak? How might that set the tone for worship?

# ACTION

MAKE A PACT WITH KEY LEADERS ON YOUR TEAM THAT YOU WON'T OFFER FEEDBACK OR CONSTRUCTIVE CRITICISM TO EACH OTHER ON SUNDAY, ESPECIALLY RIGHT BEFORE A SERVICE. COMMIT TO EACH OTHER THAT FOR THE SAKE OF TEAM UNITY, YOU WILL SAVE COMMENTS FOR ANOTHER DAY.

# 6

## CLEVER OR REAL

### RESIST THE PULL TO IMPRESS

Most weeks when I lead worship, I share a short thought somewhere in the worship set. These anecdotes have affectionately become known as "Doug's sermonettes." When people first started using this term it kind of bothered me, because I knew how much work it takes to create a real sermon. I didn't think my quick little thoughts each week were very important. But over the years, I've realized that these moments are, in fact, very memorable to the congregation and can make a great impact on people.

I'm continually asking God what He wants me to

share. I equally ask Him when I'm not supposed to share. You see, the more I started to do sermonettes, the more often I felt the pressure of needing to be clever or impressive. At times, I would get an idea and would think "Wow! This is good. The people are going to love this!"—only to watch it bomb. Other times I felt unprepared and shared something that felt (in my view) very simple and unimpressive, yet it would minister to many.

What I've found is that if I write down just a few notes and let God prompt me to expound on those notes, the outcome is better. Less clever. Less me feeling the need to impress. These notes were never complete sentences because I didn't want to sound like I was reading a script. Just a few bullet points to keep me on track. In the old days, I would write it down on a piece of paper. With the advent of the iPad and my music apps, now all this information is conveniently in front me so I don't have pages to flip through.

Personally, I get a little weirded out when I hear someone else say something along the lines of "God told me (fill in the blank)." Is it possible that person heard from God directly? Sure, but my guess is that some of us use this phrase a little too much. However, I have experienced a few times in my life where God has impressed something upon me so hard that I knew He was speaking directly to me.

Specific to worship, here is what I heard: "Come as you are. Do all that you can. Leave the results to Me."

There is so much good here. Let me see if I can unpack it a bit.

## COME AS YOU ARE

Each of us are different. This world of ours has many different music styles, a wide variety of churches, and a vast array of preferences for what a church service looks like. We certainly have many opinions on how we express ourselves as we worship. One of the things we do that often gets us sidetracked is compare ourselves to others.

Yes, you can find a healthy way to observe and to evaluate how other churches operate. But, a difference exists between studying for the sake of discussion and studying for the sake of copying. I see this compare-and-copy too often in the realm of worship. I could be wrong, but chances are God doesn't want you to identify your worship DNA by hitting "copy and paste" from the church down the road or the cool church on TV. Instead, approach your worship "as you are."

## DO ALL YOU CAN

Do everything you can with your talent, your crew, your style, and your passion, based on the people of your congregation. If you have a one-hundred-piece orchestra, use it. If you have one acoustic guitar, use it. If you have a three-hundred-person choir, use it. If you have an accordion, use it. See the point? Use what God has given you, and use it with a thankful heart. Watch what He will do, and be confident in who *you* are.

Doing all that you can also differs based on what chapter of life you are in at that specific time. Sometimes you will lead through a joyful heart. Sometimes you will lead with a broken heart. Sometimes you will be living through hope or through discouragement. God knows that. When the people you lead see you being vulnerable and authentic, they will learn to appreciate you and connect with you—and ultimately God through you—more deeply.

## LEAVE THE RESULTS TO GOD

If God were to give me a report card on this subject, I think I would get a D+. I'm not good at leaving the results to Him. I take things personally. I never take credit when we have an amazing time of worship, but on the flip side, I find myself feeling like a failure when I perceive that worship has not gone well. Bad worship experiences burn deep into my mind. They shouldn't, but they do, which is why this last phrase is so important. I find myself constantly trying to improve in this area, but I think it's a tough one for a lot of worship leaders.

These negative feelings of failure can often take days to work their way out of my thoughts. However, from experience, I can say that even when I felt like nothing had happened during worship, I have later received notes from people at church saying how much God had moved in their hearts that very day. The truth is we can never really tell with our physical eyes what God is doing in hearts during worship. We might think we know, but we can often be wrong. The results are truly His, and we are better off if we can learn to live with that reality.

To me, this old children's song expresses this concept well:

> *I'm yours Lord, everything I've got*
> *Everything I am, everything I'm not*
> *I'm yours Lord, try me now and see*
> *See if I can be completely yours*[2]

I see a lot of wisdom packed into this fun little song. To some of you this song is familiar, to some of you it is not. Let's explore that a bit–the concept of familiarity. You see, if I were to come into my church and lead a new song each week, people would be lost. Yes, the band might sound great, but my goal as a leader is not to have people watch the band, but to bring them into worship. Our goal is to lead the congregation in a way where the people take over, the voices take flight, and the band takes a backseat and just enjoys the ride. We are merely a part of the overall orchestra of souls creating an offering of worship to our Heavenly Father. Just because we're up there in the spotlight doesn't make us any more important. In fact, because the lights are on us, we must continually remind ourselves that worship is not about us: "Not to us, Lord, not to us but to your name be the glory" (Psalm 115:1).

I pray each week that God would lead me to the songs He wants, to the Scripture He wants me to share with the people. I'm mindful that for many people who come to church, that one hour (give or take) on Sunday morning is their only encounter with Christian music of any kind. What a huge responsibility! Plus, I must keep in mind that both a hymn that is two hundred years old or a song that just hit radio last week could be equally unknown to them.

I love loud music. I love quiet music. I love moving lights. I love no lights. I love modern music. I love old music. I love having lyrics on giant screens. I love singing songs from memory with no screens at all. I love the epic chug of a worship anthem as you can feel the anticipation build, as the crowd belts out the final chorus with every ounce of praise they have in them. I love the moments when you can hear a pin drop, those times when I as a worship leader cannot even sing myself because it is so beautiful to be in the splendor of God's presence.

The beauty here is not in the music itself, that people leave that day impressed by the talent of the band, but by the glory of God Himself. And that's a unicorn worth chasing.

## ACTION

THINK ABOUT ALL THE THINGS YOU'RE GOOD AT, ALL YOUR TALENTS WITH WHICH YOU'RE COMFORTABLE AND THE THINGS FOR WHICH PEOPLE COMPLIMENT YOU. NOW THINK OF ALL THE THINGS YOU'RE NOT GOOD AT, THE THINGS YOU WISH YOU COULD DO WELL, BUT FEEL LIKE YOU DON'T. IN A VERY REAL AND HONEST WAY, ASK GOD TO USE YOU, JUST THE WAY HE MADE YOU.

# 7

## THE MEMORY MAKER

### FIND MUSIC THAT YOUR CHURCH CAN OWN

Think back to your earliest memory of singing in church. You may have been a kid in children's church. You may have been 20, 40, or 60 years old the first time you set foot in a sanctuary. Whatever age you were, you likely have specific moments and memories that flood back into your mind and emotions when you hear a certain song. Music does that to us. The connection music has with memory is one reason songs are so powerful. They take us back to a season of life or even an event that altered the course of our walk from that point forward. I have certain songs that do that for me.

The other night, I was going through a hymnal picking out songs that I remember singing and that I thought still translated well into worship today. Before you get all worried that this is a "Bring back all the hymns" campaign, let me assure you it is not. But hymns impress me. Their lyrics and theology are among some of the most solid and inspiring to be found in any type of worship music. And for many people, hymns are a trigger that bring them back to a special place in their memories. I can tell you as worship leaders that this is a place we want to take people! For as long as God allows me to lead, I'll have one foot placed in the modern world and another foot placed a couple hundred years ago in some of these great hymns.

But this chapter is not about hymns alone. It's about memories. Let me explain: One day when I was planning music, I was thinking about songs that are still really special to me. Some are hundreds of years old, while others are from the 1970s, '80s, '90s, 2000s, and so on. You get the point. In your church, people will have special memories attached to a wide variety of music from a wide variety of time periods. And when you play one of their favorite songs, the music does more than just make them feel good or put a smile on their faces. The experience can move them deeply. When I pull out some of these classic songs, it means the world to some people. They respond almost as if they are saying "Thanks for not forgetting about me."

Why does this connection to memory matter? Some churches are so consumed with being modern and relevant that they have no room for songs that are just a few years old. This philosophy perplexes me on a few levels. One is the idea of "shelf life." Consider a song like "How Great Thou Art," written in 1885. This hymn has a shelf life (so far) of over one hundred years and is still going strong. Your parents sang it. Your grandparents sang it. If you were to get your whole family in a room together, you may even be able to have a beautiful multigenerational worship experience.

Contrast that with today's music. Pick your favorite song right now. Think about the song the church goes crazy for, the song that is number one on the radio. Maybe it's the one that wrecks you in your personal worship experience. Today, we are so quick to throw songs like that away. A new one will come along in six months, and we'll kick that "old" one to the curb. What we consider popular and powerful today, we might label irrelevant in a year.

Today, we have an abundance of high-quality, well-written, inspirational Christian music available, perhaps more than ever before. As a worship leader, I'm mindful that I'm the one who makes decisions that affect others. I decide which songs are sung each week. That responsibility is overwhelming at times, one that I take very seriously.

What causes me to raise a red flag of concern as a worship leader is that we could be killing potential memories. The life cycle of songs today seems to be shorter than ever. So many churches do only new music, and even within that new music, the new songs only last a short while. My fear here is that people can grow up and have no real songs they can "own" for themselves.

We are leading a generation of people who could

be singing in church twenty years after we are gone, but have no memories sparked during worship. The songs they grew up with might never be sung again. The songs that gave them a personal, powerful worship experience might never be played again. For this reason, I try to pick songs that might have better odds of having a longer shelf life.

As you evaluate your music selection, here are a few things to consider:

*Does the song sound good with a full band?*
*Does it sound good as an acoustic version?*
*Does it work loud?*
*Does it work stripped back and very soft?*
*Is the melody easy for the congregation to catch?*
*Is the vocal range attainable by most people?*

I think the more "yes" answers you have to these questions, the more likely you can still do the song in ten years, twenty years, and beyond. Let me give a few examples of songs that have done just that. I mentioned "How Great

Thou Art." But take a trip down memory lane with me and consider some of the most popular worship songs through the decades:

> *1970s: "Father I Adore You"; "Open Our Eyes, Lord"*
> *1980s: "El Shaddai"; "Lord I Lift Your Name on High"*
> *1990s: "Shout to the Lord"; "Let it Rise"*
> *2000s: "I Can Only Imagine"; "How Great is Our God"*
> *2010s: "Oceans (Where Feet May Fail)"; "10,000 Reasons (Bless The Lord)"*

Having led people for nearly thirty years now, I know people who grew up with me as their worship leader, and many of those people are still in the congregation. They might have been fifteen years old the first time we did "How Great is Our God." If I pull out that song this weekend fifteen years later, that thirty-year-old person has fond memories of singing that song for the first time when he was fifteen. The song brings back memories. It takes him back to a different place. In our case, he might remember singing that song in our old sanctuary versus our new worship center.

These memories elicit real emotion and real connection. Do we do this for the sake of emotion alone? No. But people do have feelings and emotion, which can be an indication that God is moving.

When I lead, sometimes I think I can almost see little thought bubbles above people's heads as they sing. As a shepherd to the people I lead at my church, I care about them. I care about their stories. To the extent that I can, I try to be involved in their lives and encourage them. As my church approaches a congregation of two thousand, this individual connection becomes harder and harder, but I try. If you know your people, you can be more sensitive to what translates well to them and what doesn't. You have to do more than just play your favorite songs for them; you need to find songs that speak to your people, giving them an avenue to express themselves to the Lord in worship.

If you've been leading for a while, take this challenge to heart. Pull out songs that were meaningful at one time, but they've been collecting dust for a while.

Pray about your song selection. Consider what song God might want to resurrect, even if it's only once, and see how it can impact your people.

If you're new to worship leading, consider this concept of making memories. Try to make a conscious effort to watch the songs that resonate with your church. These songs are the ones that become a rally cry for your congregation, the songs that they "own" and belt out at the top of their lungs. Don't let these songs die too soon.

There is a difference between a song a church sings and a song a church "owns." For example, some of my personal favorite songs would not necessarily translate well into a congregational setting, where the people can really grab hold of it and own it. Those moments when a song hits the mark and you can see that people have embraced it as their own—those are the moments I live for.

Though I try not to, I have no doubt I've often made the mistake of introducing songs that were more in the category of "songs I like" than "songs this church needs." Every worship leader knows his or her congregation. They know the stories of the people at the church. If they are in tune with the people they lead, they know from week to week what songs are going to glorify God and speak to the needs of their people.

Every week we as worship leaders must live in the reality that someone will like the music we do, and most likely someone will not. Welcome to music. As you prepare your worship experience for your church, both in the short-term weekly planning and in your long-range planning, ponder this: Will people ten years from now be able to relive any worship memories? Will they be able to sing a song more deeply because they don't have to rely on reading words on a screen or on a piece of paper? Will they intimately know the truth of those words, so that in those moments, their worship reaches a new level? When songs live inside of us, our worship takes on a deeper meaning, and our connection to the Lord becomes even stronger.

Each week I try to find a balance. Some loud songs, some soft songs, some fast, some slow. Everything we do from a leadership standpoint is to encourage the people to engage with God.

I often tell the band during rehearsal "We need to let the voices carry this; we are just here for support. We don't need to show off. We don't need to play loud. We don't need an extended solo, but we need to let the song spread its wings and take flight." And I love it when a song takes flight. Those moments when I see the congregation "own" a song are some of the powerful and cherished experiences of my life.

## ACTION

THINK BACK FIVE OR TEN YEARS TO A SONG THAT HELD DEEP MEANING TO YOUR CONGREGATION. PULL IT BACK OUT OF YOUR MUSIC ARCHIVES AND ADD IT TO YOUR SET LIST THIS WEEK. CONSIDER INCLUDING AN EXPLANATION ABOUT WHY YOU SELECTED IT OR WHAT YOU REMEMBER MOST ABOUT IT DURING THE SERVICE. ENJOY TAKING A TRIP DOWN MEMORY LANE WITH YOUR PEOPLE AND ENJOY WITH THEM AS YOU RELIVE THE SPECIAL MEMORY OF THAT SONG. IF YOU ARE NEW TO LEADING OR YOU HAVE A BRAND-NEW YOUNG CHURCH, YOU MAY NOT BE ABLE TO CAPTURE OLD MEMORIES, BUT YOU CAN START CREATING NEW ONES. BE MINDFUL THAT THE CHOICES YOU MAKE WILL SHAPE YOUR CONGREGATION.

# 8

# A SURE THING

UTILIZE YOUR BEST NONMUSICAL RESOURCE

Music is understandably one of our central focus points as worship leaders. We work hard for many years to sharpen our skills as musicians or vocalists. Psalm 33:3 instructs that we are to "play skillfully." Music is a beautiful part of worship, to be sure, but it's just that: a part. I have a good friend who leads a church stewardship company. He teaches on how our offering time can be a powerful time of worship, more than just dropping money in a plate as it passes along to the next person. As we listen to a sermon, we can worship. If we choose to listen to the pastor's message, letting truth impact us, thinking about what those words mean for us personally, giving all our attention to Scripture, we worship. Foundational to any worship experience, one that embodies the fullness of God, is that of God's Word—both personally and within the context of corporate worship.

## PERSONAL TIME IN THE WORD

We as believers, and certainly worship leaders, are to be in the Word. Both for our individual walk and on behalf of those we lead. If you're like most, you struggle with taking time to read the Bible. I have periods of my life when I struggle too. I look back on long stretches of time when I was faithful every day and others when I never opened the Bible for days or weeks at a time. When I'm in the Word, I win. When I ignore the Word, I lose. We all probably can relate to that and testify this truth. How then are we unmotivated? How do we become so easily distracted and find more important things to do?

When I was in college, as part of my Bible major, I had assignments that required me to be in the Word. I'm thankful for that. But looking back, I also can see how I grew callous to it. At times, God's Word was a textbook and not a life book. Sometimes when I plan worship today, I can even find myself searching more for what I can share with others, than for how it needs to impact me personally. I'm getting better, but that struggle can pop up from time to time.

As worship leaders, we are challenged to both know Christ and to make Him known. The first goal is directed at us. The second goal is directed at others. Too often I find myself driven by a desire to find something compelling to share with others. Sure, that pursuit sounds noble, but if I don't focus first on knowing Christ in a real way myself, then it's a hard jump to try to be an effective leader and convey to others how they are to know Him.

As we spend time in the Bible, we must let ourselves be impacted. Overwhelmed. Blown away. I struggle to read long passages of Scripture. I'm wired in such a way that I do much better if I read the words aloud. If I read silently, my mind tends to race ahead and lose much of what I'm reading. If this at all resonates with you, give yourself freedom to read more slowly. Be okay with reading less than you planned. Be okay with reading small chunks at a time. But let those chunks change you. If Scripture stops you dead in your tracks and you feel like you need to pray right in that moment, do it.

I once heard a pastor give a powerful illustration. He said that every day we go without spending time in the Word, it's like we look up to God, punch Him in the face, and say "I don't need You!" This metaphor really got my attention. I had never thought how it hurts God when we do nothing. But I've come to believe that it does hurt Him when we don't grow to our full potential. He wants to talk to us. He does that through music and sermons, but He also wants to spend one-on-one time with us. He wants us to invite Him to speak to us. He wants to speak to us personally. This communication with God happens when we, on our own initiative, open up the Bible and read God's Word. You can't find a substitute for this. The enemy knows the power of God's Word too, so he will always do whatever he can to distract us from reading the Bible for ourselves.

We must be in God's Word not only for us, but also for the people we are leading. The Bible is full of passages that can inspire us. It is loaded with true stories we can present to our congregations to draw them closer to the Lord or pull them into the songs we lead. Our ability to lead well makes it even more important for us to be in the Word personally. It's good to listen to it; it's beneficial to have a sermon preached to you. But you can have a much more intimate and personal experience when you sit alone, you and God, and listen to Him speak directly to you. Every day that we consciously choose to come up with some creative excuse as to why we don't have time for the Bible, we lose. Every time we push through those foolish excuses and spend time in the Bible, we win. May God forgive us for the many days we've lost. May we feel in a real, tangible way that it hurts God when we do nothing. May we be motivated to be on our knees before Him.

I've heard it said that God loves you just the way you are, but He doesn't want you to stay that way. Open up your Bible today. God is waiting to speak to you, and I guarantee you will be better for it. Time in God's Word is time well spent.

## THE WORD AS WORSHIP

Fun fact about songs: They fail. Can I get an "Amen!"? I have numerous horror stories of songs that for various reasons didn't work. As musicians, we are never guaranteed that a song will be embraced by our congregations. I've had times where I had a "sure thing"—a song that I fell in love with, was number one on the radio, and the band played skillfully. Yet, when we introduced it to the congregation, the song totally bombed, only to be blacklisted for all eternity. I've also had songs that I really questioned, because they were corny, outdated, too simple, too cheesy, too easy, or too hard. Yet, when we introduced them to the congregation, the people instantly engaged and worshiped. Sometimes we never know until we try.

But the unpredictability of songs is why I love Scripture. We have no guarantee with a song, no certainty with how it will resonate with the congregation. But with Scripture, you have a guarantee. When we share Bible verses as a part of worship, we can bet the farm that the Word will never return void. Isaiah 55:11 says,

> *So is my word that goes out from my mouth:*
> *It will not return to me empty,*
> *but will accomplish what I desire*
> *and achieve the purpose for which I sent it.*

Do we really believe that? That God's Word will always go out and accomplish what it is meant to do? If you ever attended a service at my church, most likely you will hear me share Scripture. It's something I can bank on. Is it worth giving up a three-minute song slot in the worship set to read three minutes of Scripture? Absolutely! I can know with one-hundred percent certainty that when I share a passage of Scripture it will go out and accomplish what God wants it to do on that particular day. I may receive confirmation on that special verse the same day, the next week, or never at all. But I can believe with total faith and the utmost confidence that God's Word will go out and minister to the hearts of the people who hear it.

It will never return void. We can have full assurance of that.

If you ever feel the struggle of "I don't want to lose a song to read a Bible verse," let me challenge you with this: Music is not worship. Let me say again: music is not worship. Can music be worship? Absolutely. Can music not be worship? Yep. (See Chapter 1.) In some Christian circles, we have blended music and worship into the same thing, but it is not. As a musician, of course music is dear to my heart and I believe it is one of the most powerful ways we can worship. But—and this is a *monumental* distinction—music is not the only way. As we read Scripture, as we listen to sermons, as we pray, as we serve others, and as we give, all these actions can be acts of worship. Let's not forget that.

## CONNECTING SCRIPTURE AND SONGS

Hopefully in your church many of the songs you sing are based on Scripture. In some cases, songs are taken word for word from the Bible. While I love this for the sake of theological accuracy, I have to remind myself that sometimes we sing lyrics that need to be explained to people. We should never assume everyone in our congregation grew up in the church or understands everything we sing. In many growing churches, quite the opposite is true. And so it is vital that we take the time to explain phrases and concepts and unique words to our people.

Let me give you an example. You probably know the song "Come Thou Fount of Every Blessing." It's a well-known song with a familiar melody. You've probably sang it multiple times. Many people have. I sang it for years as a kid. Eventually as a worship leader, I also led the song. One day it struck me: What on earth does "here I raise my Ebenezer" mean? What is an *Ebenezer*? My only experience with that particular word was from the old grumpy guy in *A Christmas Carol*. I was pretty sure this song wasn't about him.

I took it upon myself to do some research one day and learn about it. In 1 Samuel 7, after the Israelite victory, the Bible records: "Then Samuel took a stone and set it up between Mizpah and Shen. He named it Ebenezer, saying, 'Thus far the LORD has helped us' " (v. 12).

The word *Ebenezer* simply means "stone of help." An Ebenezer, then, is a monumental stone set up to signify the great help that God granted the one raising the stone. When we sing the song, we acknowledge God's bountiful blessings and help in our lives. As you sing about raising your Ebenezer, you are saying, "God I acknowledge your help in my life."

Once I understood this lyric, the next time we did the song in church, I took a couple minutes to teach the congregation the meaning of the word *Ebenezer* and the meaning of that verse. You can imagine that when we then sang the song, it took on a whole new level of connection with the people. They now understood what they were singing.

Another extremely popular song right now, "Reckless Love," talks about the love of God. It has a lyric: "Oh, it chases me down, fights 'til I'm found, leaves the ninety-nine." You've probably heard it. I love the music and the power of the song, but I also realized some people have no idea what ninety-nine things were left.

Again, I did some homework. For perspective, I

watched a few interviews with the composer, and the first time we introduced this song, I took some time to read the passage from Luke 15. I talked about how Jesus is the Shepherd and He cares so much for the individual, that like a shepherd, He would leave the ninety-nine sheep that are not lost to find the one that is lost. Taking a few minutes to explain that phrase took the song to a new level. People can sing the lyric and it now means something to them personally. Had I skipped the intro, people may have sang, but not everyone would have made the connection.

**ALWAYS BE WILLING TO TAKE TIME TO TEACH THE PEOPLE YOU LEAD.**

## ACTION

FIND A BIBLE VERSE THAT GOES ALONG WITH A SONG YOU LEAD THIS WEEK. SHARE IT WITH THE CONGREGATION. IN ADDITION TO READING IT, SHARE WHAT IT MEANS TO YOU PERSONALLY. IN YOUR OWN WORDS, LET THE PEOPLE HEAR FROM YOUR HEART HOW THIS PASSAGE RELATES TO THE SONG AND HOW IT CAN IMPACT THEIR LIVES.

# 9

## DOGS AND CATS

### DON'T BE THE FOOLISH ANIMAL

I'm a dog person. Let me confess that right off the bat. And before you wonder "I thought this was a worship book?"—stick with me for a minute. At our house, we have two inside dogs, two inside cats, and a plethora of outside cats whose exact quantity varies with the seasons. None of these outside cats belong to us, but we've discovered that if you put out food, cats stick around. And multiply.

Inside the house, the Hood cat farm consists of just two members: Molly and Jax. Molly was found as a newborn alone in our backyard and nursed back to health. She was once a scrawny, undernourished little kitten. Today she is, shall we say, well nourished. If there is a relationship ratio between happiness and size, Molly is *very* happy. Then we have Jax, who showed up at our house one Thanksgiving inside the engine block of a car in our driveway. After hours of tedious extraction work by my clever wife and daughters, little Jax was rescued and came inside to live with us.

In our dog department, we have a small, brown, long-haired dachshund named Dawson, and a rather large black Newfoundland named Bear. Each dog is not aware of his size. We think each believes he is a regular-size dog, but neither is. As you can imagine, we always have some interesting pet activity going on at our house.

Although I already revealed my bias towards dogs, I know cat people are out there so let me try and find common ground with you. I like cats. I do. They are entertaining to watch, and they definitely take care of themselves much better than a dog. You can leave them alone for days at a time, and they do their thing and take care of their business, which dogs cannot. (At least not inside the house.)

But, to me, a dog is your buddy. A dog shows you affection. A dog is crazy happy to see you when you come home each day. You can teach a dog tricks. So clearly the dog is superior, right?

Yet, as much as I love dogs, dogs do one thing that is not admirable. Are you ready for it? If you're eating right now, please come back and visit this chapter later. Here it comes (you've been warned): A dog will eat its vomit. Yummy, right? As if vomit is not gross enough on its own, the thought of going back and eating it is truly disgusting. We as educated, smart, intelligent people, would look at that and say "That dog is dumb. I'm not dumb. I would never be like a dog." But sometimes we are like a dog. The Bible says so: "As a dog returns to its vomit, so a fool repeats his foolishness" (Prov. 26:11 NLT).

What does this verse teach us? If we continue doing the same foolish things over and over, we are like a dog going back and eating its own vomit. It's gross (super gross) and just plain dumb.

If you're reading this book, you are at least open to the idea of looking for ways you can be more effective in worship, in teaching, in collaborating with your team, and in better leading the people of your church. Most likely you can already look back on the things you've done, the experiences you've had, and see areas where you have been foolish. That is normal. Don't beat yourself up too much over the past. But my encouragement and challenge to you from Proverbs is this: Don't *repeat* your foolishness. Don't keep on doing things that hurt you or that don't accomplish any good.

Here's an example how I've been a dog. I know that a congregation can handle only a limited amount of new music. Let's face it, if we do five new songs a week for fifty-two weeks a year, our people will just be overloaded. Throughout the year, almost monthly, new worship music is released. As musicians, we love this. As leaders, we will latch on to some songs and think "This will be perfect for my church!" But even so, I've learned not to do more than one unfamiliar song during a worship set.

However, some weeks I'm bombarded with requests for the hot song of the day, and I can set aside wisdom in pursuit of popularity. In fact, I've found myself in the middle of a worship set thinking to myself "You've done it again. You have too many new songs here." I've seen what happens when I have included too many songs people don't know. It's a quick service-killer. People mentally check out. They are not engaged. Yet, for the sake of my love for a song, and the quest to be on the cutting edge of the "flavor of the week," I can give in and return to my foolishness. I become the dog.

The worship unicorn is not found in a magic pill. True, authentic, engaging worship is not lightning in a bottle, and you cannot find a scripted formula to follow. You cannot achieve it by a potion or by following a mathematical formula that yields predictable results. It's the pursuit of what is possible, of what God can do when we give Him our hearts and voices. Sometimes our worship services feel alive. Sometimes they feel dead. But we cannot rely on feelings.

That worship unicorn shows up when we are reminded who God is and realize how awesome a privilege we have to experience Him in worship. Worship can happen in a huge cathedral or a tent. It can be facilitated by a group of world-class musicians or a single volunteer struggling to lead the best she can. It occurs in highly organized churches with multimillion-dollar budgets and the poorest of the poor. In all these extremes, authenticity is paramount.

At my church, the services that were the most powerful were those that had incredible times of authentic, honest, engaging worship. You know, the ones where you look out at a sea of people and witness faces that are truly experiencing the Lord. How can you be in settings like that and not be moved? In those moments, music and lyrics are transcended, and the church is fully immersed in the presence of Almighty God.

After a service like that, in my humanness, I easily ponder "Okay, let's figure out how we did that and hit the repeat button!" But inherent in that thought is the false assumption that we created that experience. We didn't. God let us into that moment. When I try to recreate it on my own strength, I am the dog.

You will not find the worship unicorn by repeating what's not working or by allowing pride, fear of change, or tradition for the sake of tradition become the stopgap between you and leading God's people to His throne. You will not find the worship unicorn by copying the popular church in town or the church on TV. Instead, crack open your spiritual ears and eyes and be on the lookout for what He wants you to learn. Be willing to leave behind those habits or practices that just aren't good for you or the people you are leading.

And remember the dog.

# ACTION

WHAT IS SOMETHING FOOLISH THAT YOU RECOGNIZE IN YOURSELF AS A LEADER? MORE SPECIFICALLY, WHAT IS SOME ASPECT OF YOUR PLANNING OR LEADING THAT YOU KNOW YOU SHOULDN'T BE REPEATING? AS A LEADER, DO YOU DO ANYTHING OUT OF HABIT THAT YOU KNOW IS FOOLISH, BUT THAT YOU KEEP DOING BECAUSE IT HAS BECOME COMFORTABLE AND FAMILIAR? WRITE THESE THINGS DOWN, AND POST THEM SOMEWHERE PREVALENT. THAT WAY, WHEN YOU BEGIN PLANNING YOUR NEXT SERVICE, YOU WILL BE REMINDED NOT TO RETURN TO YOUR OLD WAYS.

# 10

## YOUR MISSION

### LEAD OTHERS IN WORSHIP

Time after time, I'm impressed the most with people who shouldn't worship, but they do. These people have every reason not to worship. The lady who buried her husband the day before. The person who received the cancer diagnosis. The man who lost his job after twenty-five years. The lady whose husband beats her. The kid who is trying to understand why his parents are getting a divorce. The girl who lost her brother to suicide. All these things happen to real people. And God puts these real people in front of us every weekend.

Any time we gather for worship, it is never "just

another" service. It might be life and death for someone. Just a couple weeks ago a man came into one of our services with his granddaughter. He was mad. To be more specific, he was mad at God. He came to church that day not for himself, but for his granddaughter. It was later shared with me that during worship, this grandfather couldn't explain what happened, but he felt something in the room as we sang. His anger melted. All the bitterness and hate to which he was holding so tightly slowly unraveled. He didn't even realize how heavy a burden he had been carrying, but he felt it lighten that day. This is what happens when we worship. This is the potential for worship. The next time you lead, it could be a day when someone decides if they give up on God or if they hold out hope for one more day. The answer they are looking for, the hope they are wishing for, could be found in one of the songs you pick.

Jaimee had been praying for a specific request for quite some time. Worn out and weary, she continued to pray faithfully. She was determined to praise God through her struggle, and she asked God for a sign. One

Sunday morning she woke up with the song "What A Beautiful Name" stuck in her head. "If we sing this in church today, I will freak out" she told her husband that morning. I had never met Jaimee, and we had never done this song before. But on that day, the last song of the worship set was indeed "her" song. After the service, she came up to the front of the stage and met me and began to tell me her story. I was again in awe of how God orchestrated these details.

For reasons like this, we should be in prayer over our song choices—not just picking songs that we like, that have a killer guitar solo, or that we think make us sound good. Prayer is so important. Hopefully we do enjoy the songs and they do sound good. But I've had numerous times when I picked an oddball song and couldn't explain why. While doing the planning, I was not sure how it would fit, and I didn't know who it was for, but I had the overwhelming assurance in my gut that God wanted me to do it.

As we did "What A Beautiful Name" that day, Jaimee told me she was overwhelmed and began to cry. She didn't cry as someone who was sad, but as someone who realized God would deliver her from her burden. Again, we had never done that song before. I had never met Jaimee.

She told me that day "This isn't about me; this is about our God and what He can do. Whatever it is, God hears you. You are not alone. Keep praying; keep believing; keep praising Him." God was orchestrating everything for that day.

## HE IS THE CONDUCTOR. HE IS THE COMPOSER.
## WE ARE MEMBERS OF THE ORCHESTRA.

A few years back, my company was a corporate sponsor for our local Christian radio station WBCL. Because of that sponsorship, we had a few perks. One day someone from the station called me and asked, "Would you be interested in a pair of front row tickets to see Kari Jobe?" After a quick two seconds, I said "Umm, yeah!" Like most of you, I love her worship music, but I had not seen her in person, so I was really looking forward to the concert. My daughter Kendall, also a big fan and member of our worship team, was my date for the evening. We settled into our front-row seats excited for the event.

Toward the end of the concert, Kari invited all the youth in the room to come up front close to the stage for the final few songs. We were at a large church with a sizable front altar area, so there was maybe twenty feet in between our front row seats and the front edge of the stage. With Kari's invitation, soon this empty space was flooded with people all around us. We continued to sing, and it was powerful to see so many people engaged in worship.

To the left of me, actually only a few inches away, was a young girl singing with all her might. If I had to guess she was maybe fifteen years old. She knew every song. She sang every word. The words were on the screens, but she was singing deeper than that. Some of the songs I didn't know, and since I'm in the "worship business," I wondered how this young girl knew all the songs so well.

Close to the girl was a woman I presumed to be her mother. The mom stood right behind her with both hands on the girl's shoulders and her head resting on the girl's left shoulder. At first, I didn't think too much about it because the place was quite crowded and people were packed in pretty tightly. But then I noticed something in the girl's hand: a collapsible cane with red and white sections. The girl was blind. The inquisitive part of me thought again, "Wait a minute. How does she know all these songs?" I looked back at the mom, and I could see why her head was resting on the girl's shoulder. She was whispering the lyrics of the songs to her daughter, leading her daughter in worship. The scene was overwhelming.

Do you remember how I said I get weirded out when people say "God spoke to me about (fill in the blank)..."? Well, on this night, I can tell you God spoke to me. Here's what He said as I looked at the mom and daughter: "This is what you do. You lead others in worship."

This image of mother and daughter became a picture of worship I hope I never forget. When I share this story even now, I become deeply overwhelmed.

I pray this can be an impacting image for you too, because this is what we do. We have the amazing privilege to point other people in God's direction. We help turn their thoughts toward Him. We tell them stories that can cause them to think about the Lord. We share things going on in our lives in the hope that the Holy Spirit can anoint our efforts and draw people heavenward.

### YOU ARE THE LIFELINE WHERE MUSIC AND MESSAGES FLOW.

Let me encourage you wherever you find yourself at this very moment. You may be in a large facility with a big staff, a huge pool of musicians, and an ample worship budget. Be thankful for those resources, and do all you can do with what you have. You may find yourself in a one-room facility, or maybe it's not even a facility at all.

Worship at your church could be you alone with your voice and a guitar or a keyboard. In addition to leading worship, you may also wear the hat of audio/visual tech or youth pastor or maybe even senior pastor. You may have no budget, no other musicians to help you, and you feel like everything falls on your shoulders. Be thankful for that, and do all you can do with what you have.

Don't ever underestimate the importance of what you do. You are not just playing songs. You are leading worship. You are leading others in worship. You are a worship leader!

## ACTION

BE ENCOURAGED. POINT AS MANY PEOPLE TO THE LORD AS YOU CAN. GIVE GOD ALL YOU'VE GOT. HOLD NOTHING BACK. LET YOUR AMBITION FOR SOULS FAR ECLIPSE YOUR DESIRE FOR MUSICAL PERFECTION. BE JOYFUL KNOWING THAT GOD IS CHEERING YOU ON—AND CHASE THAT UNICORN.

# NOTES

[1] Biography.com Editors. "Vincent van Gogh Biography." *Biography.com*. A&E Television Networks. April 2, 2014. Last modified February 5, 2019. Accessed February 9, 2019 at https://www.biography.com/people/vincent-van-gogh-9515695.

[2] Gary Chapman. "I'm Yours, Lord." Paragon Music Corporation (Admin. Music Services), 1979.

Manufactured by Amazon.ca
Bolton, ON